50 Mexican BBQ and Beyond Recipes

By: Kelly Johnson

Table of Contents

- Carne Asada (Grilled Steak)
- Pollo Asado (Grilled Chicken)
- Al Pastor Tacos (Grilled Pork)
- Grilled Barbacoa Beef
- Birria de Res (Smoky Braised Beef)
- Mexican-Style Pork Ribs (Costillas Asadas)
- Tacos de Arrachera (Skirt Steak Tacos)
- Pescado Zarandeado (Grilled Whole Fish)
- Grilled Shrimp al Mojo de Ajo
- Grilled Octopus (Pulpo a las Brasas)
- Grilled Chorizo with Peppers
- Mexican Street Corn (Elotes)
- Esquites (Mexican Corn Salad)
- Grilled Cactus (Nopales Asados)
- Charred Salsa Roja
- Fire-Roasted Salsa Verde
- Smoked Chipotle BBQ Sauce
- Grilled Queso Fundido with Chorizo
- Grilled Jalapeño Poppers (Rellenos de Queso)
- Tlayuda (Mexican Grilled Pizza)
- Grilled Tostadas with Refried Beans
- Chiles Toreados (Grilled Spicy Peppers)
- Grilled Ceviche de Camarón
- Smoked Carnitas
- Lamb Barbacoa (Slow-Pit Roasted Lamb)
- Grilled Mahi-Mahi Tacos
- Grilled Chicken Fajitas
- Grilled Vegetable Fajitas
- Costillas de Puerco en Adobo (Pork Ribs in Adobo Sauce)
- Cochinita Pibil (Smoked Yucatán Pork)
- Grilled Tlacoyos with Beans
- Carne Tampiqueña (Grilled Steak with Cheese Enchilada)
- Grilled Poblano Peppers Stuffed with Cheese
- Mexican-Style Hot Dogs (Sonoran Dogs)
- Smoked Guacamole

- Grilled Avocados with Lime and Salt
- Fire-Roasted Tomatillo Guacamole
- Grilled Cabbage Slaw with Lime Dressing
- Grilled Pineapple with Tajín
- Barbacoa Tacos with Handmade Tortillas
- Quesabirria Tacos (Grilled Birria Tacos with Cheese)
- Grilled Chicken Wings with Chipotle-Lime Glaze
- Mexican BBQ Pork Belly Burnt Ends
- Fire-Roasted Chile Relleno
- Smoked Mexican Chorizo Burgers
- Grilled Sweet Potatoes with Agave Glaze
- Grilled Watermelon with Chili and Lime
- Slow-Smoked Beef Short Ribs with Mexican Spices
- Grilled Mexican Churros
- Fire-Roasted Plantains with Dulce de Leche

Carne Asada (Grilled Steak)

Ingredients:

- 2 lbs (900g) skirt or flank steak
- ¼ cup (60ml) lime juice
- ¼ cup (60ml) orange juice
- ¼ cup (60ml) olive oil
- 2 cloves garlic, minced
- 1 teaspoon cumin
- 1 teaspoon salt
- ½ teaspoon black pepper

Instructions:

1. Mix marinade ingredients and coat steak. Marinate for at least 2 hours.
2. Grill over high heat for 4-5 minutes per side.
3. Rest for 5 minutes, then slice against the grain.

Pollo Asado (Grilled Chicken)

Ingredients:

- 2 lbs (900g) bone-in chicken thighs
- ¼ cup (60ml) lime juice
- ¼ cup (60ml) orange juice
- 1 tablespoon achiote paste
- 2 cloves garlic, minced
- 1 teaspoon oregano
- 1 teaspoon cumin
- ½ teaspoon salt

Instructions:

1. Mix marinade ingredients and coat chicken. Marinate for at least 2 hours.
2. Grill over medium heat for 6-7 minutes per side until fully cooked.

Al Pastor Tacos (Grilled Pork)

Ingredients:

- 2 lbs (900g) pork shoulder, thinly sliced
- 3 dried guajillo chiles, deseeded
- 2 dried ancho chiles, deseeded
- 2 chipotle chiles in adobo
- ½ cup (120ml) pineapple juice
- ¼ cup (60ml) white vinegar
- 2 cloves garlic
- 1 teaspoon cumin
- 1 teaspoon oregano
- ½ teaspoon salt
- 1 cup pineapple chunks

Instructions:

1. Blend marinade ingredients and coat pork. Marinate overnight.
2. Grill over medium heat, flipping occasionally, until caramelized.
3. Serve in tortillas with pineapple chunks.

Grilled Barbacoa Beef

Ingredients:

- 3 lbs (1.3kg) beef chuck roast
- 3 dried guajillo chiles, deseeded
- 2 dried ancho chiles, deseeded
- 2 cloves garlic
- 1 teaspoon cumin
- 1 teaspoon oregano
- ½ cup (120ml) vinegar
- 1 cup (240ml) beef broth
- ½ teaspoon salt

Instructions:

1. Blend chiles, garlic, cumin, oregano, vinegar, broth, and salt.
2. Coat beef with marinade and wrap in banana leaves or foil.
3. Grill over indirect heat for 3-4 hours until tender.

Birria de Res (Smoky Braised Beef)

Ingredients:

- 3 lbs (1.3kg) beef short ribs or chuck
- 3 dried guajillo chiles, deseeded
- 2 dried ancho chiles, deseeded
- 2 cloves garlic
- 1 teaspoon cumin
- 1 teaspoon oregano
- ½ teaspoon cinnamon
- 2 cups (480ml) beef broth
- 1 teaspoon salt

Instructions:

1. Blend chiles, garlic, spices, and broth.
2. Marinate beef overnight.
3. Grill or braise for 4 hours until tender.
4. Shred and serve in tacos or consommé.

Mexican-Style Pork Ribs (Costillas Asadas)

Ingredients:

- 2 lbs (900g) pork ribs
- ¼ cup (60ml) lime juice
- 2 cloves garlic, minced
- 1 teaspoon cumin
- 1 teaspoon paprika
- ½ teaspoon salt

Instructions:

1. Marinate ribs for 4 hours.
2. Grill over low heat for 1 ½ - 2 hours, flipping occasionally.
3. Serve with salsa or chimichurri.

Tacos de Arrachera (Skirt Steak Tacos)

Ingredients:

- 2 lbs (900g) skirt steak
- ¼ cup (60ml) lime juice
- 2 cloves garlic, minced
- 1 teaspoon cumin
- ½ teaspoon black pepper
- ½ teaspoon salt

Instructions:

1. Marinate steak for at least 2 hours.
2. Grill over high heat for 4-5 minutes per side.
3. Slice and serve in tortillas with salsa and guacamole.

Pescado Zarandeado (Grilled Whole Fish)

Ingredients:

- 1 whole fish (snapper or sea bass), cleaned
- ¼ cup (60ml) lime juice
- 2 tablespoons achiote paste
- 1 teaspoon oregano
- ½ teaspoon salt
- ½ teaspoon black pepper

Instructions:

1. Score fish and marinate for 2 hours.
2. Grill over medium heat for 7-8 minutes per side.
3. Serve with tortillas and salsa.

Grilled Shrimp al Mojo de Ajo

Ingredients:

- 1 lb (450g) shrimp, peeled
- 4 cloves garlic, minced
- 2 tablespoons butter
- 2 tablespoons lime juice
- ½ teaspoon salt
- ½ teaspoon paprika

Instructions:

1. Sauté garlic in butter until golden.
2. Toss shrimp with lime juice, salt, and paprika.
3. Grill for 2-3 minutes per side, then brush with garlic butter.

Grilled Octopus (Pulpo a las Brasas)

Ingredients:

- 1 lb (450g) octopus, cleaned
- ¼ cup (60ml) lime juice
- 1 teaspoon paprika
- ½ teaspoon salt
- 2 tablespoons olive oil

Instructions:

1. Boil octopus for 45 minutes until tender, then cool.
2. Marinate in lime juice, paprika, salt, and oil for 30 minutes.
3. Grill over high heat for 2-3 minutes per side.

Grilled Chorizo with Peppers

Ingredients:

- 1 lb (450g) fresh chorizo sausages
- 1 red bell pepper, sliced
- 1 green bell pepper, sliced
- 1 onion, sliced

Instructions:

1. Grill chorizo over medium heat for 12-15 minutes, turning occasionally.
2. Grill bell peppers and onion until soft.
3. Slice chorizo and serve with grilled vegetables.

Mexican Street Corn (Elotes)

Ingredients:

- 4 ears of corn, husked
- ½ cup (120g) mayonnaise
- ½ cup (120g) crumbled cotija cheese
- 1 teaspoon chili powder
- 1 lime, cut into wedges

Instructions:

1. Grill corn over medium heat until charred, about 10 minutes.
2. Spread with mayonnaise and roll in cotija cheese.
3. Sprinkle with chili powder and serve with lime wedges.

Esquites (Mexican Corn Salad)

Ingredients:

- 2 cups (300g) corn kernels
- 1 tablespoon butter
- ½ cup (120g) mayonnaise
- ½ cup (120g) crumbled cotija cheese
- 1 teaspoon chili powder
- 1 lime, juiced

Instructions:

1. Sauté corn in butter until lightly charred.
2. Mix with mayonnaise, cotija cheese, chili powder, and lime juice.

Grilled Cactus (Nopales Asados)

Ingredients:

- 4 nopales (cactus paddles), cleaned
- 1 tablespoon olive oil
- ½ teaspoon salt
- ½ teaspoon black pepper

Instructions:

1. Brush nopales with olive oil and season with salt and pepper.
2. Grill for 5 minutes per side until tender.

Charred Salsa Roja

Ingredients:

- 4 Roma tomatoes
- 2 jalapeños
- 1 small onion, halved
- 2 cloves garlic
- ½ teaspoon salt
- ¼ cup (15g) chopped cilantro

Instructions:

1. Grill tomatoes, jalapeños, onion, and garlic until charred.
2. Blend with salt and cilantro until smooth.

Fire-Roasted Salsa Verde

Ingredients:

- 5 tomatillos, husked
- 2 serrano chiles
- 1 small onion, halved
- 2 cloves garlic
- ½ teaspoon salt
- ¼ cup (15g) chopped cilantro

Instructions:

1. Grill tomatillos, chiles, onion, and garlic until charred.
2. Blend with salt and cilantro until smooth.

Smoked Chipotle BBQ Sauce

Ingredients:

- 1 cup (240ml) ketchup
- 2 chipotle peppers in adobo, minced
- ¼ cup (60ml) apple cider vinegar
- 2 tablespoons honey
- 1 teaspoon cumin
- 1 teaspoon smoked paprika

Instructions:

1. Simmer all ingredients for 10 minutes, stirring occasionally.
2. Let cool and blend for a smoother texture.

Grilled Queso Fundido with Chorizo

Ingredients:

- 2 cups (200g) shredded Oaxaca or Monterey Jack cheese
- ½ cup (100g) cooked chorizo
- 1 small onion, chopped
- 1 small poblano pepper, roasted and chopped

Instructions:

1. Preheat grill to medium heat.
2. Layer cheese, chorizo, onion, and poblano in a grill-safe dish.
3. Grill for 10 minutes until cheese melts. Serve with tortillas.

Grilled Jalapeño Poppers (Rellenos de Queso)

Ingredients:

- 8 large jalapeños
- ½ cup (120g) cream cheese
- ½ cup (120g) shredded cheddar
- ½ teaspoon garlic powder
- 8 slices bacon (optional)

Instructions:

1. Slice jalapeños lengthwise and remove seeds.
2. Mix cream cheese, cheddar, and garlic powder, then fill jalapeños.
3. Wrap in bacon if desired, then grill for 5-7 minutes per side.

Tlayuda (Mexican Grilled Pizza)

Ingredients:

- 1 large tlayuda tortilla (or extra-large corn tortilla)
- ½ cup (120g) refried black beans
- ½ cup (120g) shredded Oaxaca cheese
- ½ cup (75g) shredded cabbage
- 1 avocado, sliced
- ½ cup (120g) cooked chorizo

Instructions:

1. Grill tortilla until crispy.
2. Spread refried beans, then top with cheese, cabbage, avocado, and chorizo.
3. Serve open-faced or folded.

Grilled Tostadas with Refried Beans

Ingredients:

- 4 corn tortillas
- 1 cup (240g) refried beans
- ½ cup (120g) shredded cheese
- ½ cup (75g) shredded lettuce

Instructions:

1. Grill tortillas until crispy.
2. Spread refried beans and sprinkle with cheese.
3. Top with lettuce and serve.

Chiles Toreados (Grilled Spicy Peppers)

Ingredients:

- 6 serrano or jalapeño peppers
- 1 tablespoon olive oil
- ½ teaspoon salt

Instructions:

1. Toss peppers in olive oil and salt.
2. Grill over high heat until blistered.

Grilled Ceviche de Camarón

Ingredients:

- 1 lb (450g) shrimp, peeled
- ¼ cup (60ml) lime juice
- 1 small red onion, finely chopped
- 1 tomato, diced
- 1 jalapeño, chopped
- ¼ cup (15g) chopped cilantro
- ½ teaspoon salt

Instructions:

1. Grill shrimp for 2-3 minutes per side.
2. Chop shrimp and mix with lime juice, onion, tomato, jalapeño, cilantro, and salt.
3. Let sit for 15 minutes before serving.

Smoked Carnitas

Ingredients:

- 4 lbs (1.8kg) pork shoulder, cut into large chunks
- ¼ cup (60ml) orange juice
- ¼ cup (60ml) lime juice
- 1 tablespoon salt
- 1 teaspoon cumin
- 1 teaspoon smoked paprika
- 1 teaspoon black pepper

Instructions:

1. Preheat smoker to 250°F (120°C).
2. Rub pork with salt, cumin, paprika, and black pepper.
3. Smoke for 4-5 hours, spritzing with orange and lime juice every hour.
4. Shred and sear in a hot pan before serving.

Lamb Barbacoa (Slow-Pit Roasted Lamb)

Ingredients:

- 4 lbs (1.8kg) lamb shoulder or leg
- 3 dried guajillo chiles, deseeded
- 2 dried ancho chiles, deseeded
- 2 cloves garlic
- 1 teaspoon cumin
- 1 teaspoon oregano
- ½ cup (120ml) vinegar
- 1 teaspoon salt
- Banana leaves (optional)

Instructions:

1. Blend soaked chiles, garlic, cumin, oregano, vinegar, and salt into a paste.
2. Coat lamb and marinate overnight.
3. Wrap in banana leaves, place in a smoker or pit at 275°F (135°C) for 6 hours.
4. Shred and serve with tortillas.

Grilled Mahi-Mahi Tacos

Ingredients:

- 1 lb (450g) mahi-mahi fillets
- 2 tablespoons lime juice
- 1 teaspoon chili powder
- ½ teaspoon salt
- ½ teaspoon black pepper
- 8 corn tortillas

Instructions:

1. Marinate fish with lime juice, chili powder, salt, and pepper for 30 minutes.
2. Grill over medium heat for 3-4 minutes per side.
3. Serve in tortillas with slaw and salsa.

Grilled Chicken Fajitas

Ingredients:

- 2 lbs (900g) chicken breasts or thighs
- 1 teaspoon cumin
- 1 teaspoon chili powder
- ½ teaspoon garlic powder
- ½ teaspoon salt
- ½ teaspoon black pepper
- 1 red bell pepper, sliced
- 1 green bell pepper, sliced
- 1 onion, sliced

Instructions:

1. Season chicken with spices and grill over medium heat for 6-7 minutes per side.
2. Sauté bell peppers and onion in a grill pan.
3. Slice chicken and serve with tortillas.

Grilled Vegetable Fajitas

Ingredients:

- 1 zucchini, sliced
- 1 red bell pepper, sliced
- 1 yellow bell pepper, sliced
- 1 onion, sliced
- 1 teaspoon cumin
- ½ teaspoon salt
- 2 tablespoons olive oil

Instructions:

1. Toss vegetables with olive oil, cumin, and salt.
2. Grill over medium heat until charred.
3. Serve with tortillas and guacamole.

Costillas de Puerco en Adobo (Pork Ribs in Adobo Sauce)

Ingredients:

- 2 lbs (900g) pork ribs
- 3 dried guajillo chiles, deseeded
- 2 dried ancho chiles, deseeded
- 2 cloves garlic
- 1 teaspoon cumin
- ½ teaspoon salt
- ¼ cup (60ml) vinegar
- 1 teaspoon oregano

Instructions:

1. Blend soaked chiles, garlic, cumin, salt, vinegar, and oregano into a paste.
2. Coat ribs and marinate overnight.
3. Grill over low heat for 2 hours, basting with marinade.

Cochinita Pibil (Smoked Yucatán Pork)

Ingredients:

- 4 lbs (1.8kg) pork shoulder
- ½ cup (120ml) orange juice
- ¼ cup (60ml) lime juice
- ¼ cup (60ml) white vinegar
- 3 tablespoons achiote paste
- 1 teaspoon cumin
- 1 teaspoon oregano
- ½ teaspoon salt
- Banana leaves (optional)

Instructions:

1. Blend marinade ingredients and coat pork. Marinate overnight.
2. Wrap in banana leaves and smoke at 275°F (135°C) for 5 hours.
3. Shred and serve in tacos with pickled onions.

Grilled Tlacoyos with Beans

Ingredients:

- 2 cups (250g) masa harina
- 1 cup (240ml) warm water
- ½ teaspoon salt
- 1 cup (240g) refried beans

Instructions:

1. Mix masa, water, and salt into a dough.
2. Shape into oval patties and fill with beans.
3. Grill over medium heat until crispy.

Carne Tampiqueña (Grilled Steak with Cheese Enchilada)

Ingredients:

- 2 lbs (900g) skirt steak
- 1 teaspoon cumin
- 1 teaspoon garlic powder
- ½ teaspoon salt
- ½ teaspoon black pepper
- 4 cheese enchiladas

Instructions:

1. Season steak and grill over high heat for 5 minutes per side.
2. Serve with cheese enchiladas and guacamole.

Grilled Poblano Peppers Stuffed with Cheese

Ingredients:

- 4 poblano peppers
- 1 cup (120g) shredded Oaxaca cheese
- ½ teaspoon salt

Instructions:

1. Grill poblanos until charred, then peel.
2. Stuff with cheese, secure with toothpicks, and grill for 3 minutes per side.

Mexican-Style Hot Dogs (Sonoran Dogs)

Ingredients:

- 4 hot dog sausages
- 4 slices bacon
- 4 bolillo rolls
- ½ cup (75g) diced tomatoes
- ¼ cup (30g) chopped onions
- ¼ cup (30g) chopped jalapeños
- ¼ cup (60ml) mayonnaise

Instructions:

1. Wrap hot dogs in bacon and grill until crispy.
2. Serve in bolillo rolls with toppings and mayonnaise.

Smoked Guacamole

Ingredients:

- 3 ripe avocados, halved and pitted
- 2 Roma tomatoes, halved
- 1 jalapeño, halved
- ½ red onion, quartered
- 2 cloves garlic, unpeeled
- 1 tablespoon olive oil
- ½ teaspoon salt
- ¼ cup (15g) chopped cilantro
- 1 lime, juiced

Instructions:

1. Preheat smoker to 225°F (107°C).
2. Brush avocados, tomatoes, jalapeño, onion, and garlic with olive oil and sprinkle with salt.
3. Smoke for 30 minutes.
4. Scoop avocado into a bowl, peel garlic, and mash all ingredients together with lime juice and cilantro.

Grilled Avocados with Lime and Salt

Ingredients:

- 2 ripe avocados, halved and pitted
- 1 tablespoon olive oil
- ½ teaspoon sea salt
- 1 lime, cut into wedges

Instructions:

1. Brush avocado halves with olive oil.
2. Grill cut-side down over medium heat for 2-3 minutes until charred.
3. Sprinkle with salt and serve with lime wedges.

Fire-Roasted Tomatillo Guacamole

Ingredients:

- 4 tomatillos, husked
- 2 avocados, pitted
- 1 jalapeño, halved
- ½ red onion, quartered
- 2 cloves garlic
- ¼ cup (15g) chopped cilantro
- ½ teaspoon salt
- 1 lime, juiced

Instructions:

1. Grill tomatillos, jalapeño, onion, and garlic until charred.
2. Blend grilled ingredients until slightly chunky.
3. Mash with avocados, salt, lime juice, and cilantro.

Grilled Cabbage Slaw with Lime Dressing

Ingredients:

- ½ head green cabbage, quartered
- ½ red onion, sliced
- 1 carrot, shredded
- ¼ cup (15g) chopped cilantro
- 2 tablespoons olive oil
- 1 lime, juiced
- ½ teaspoon salt

Instructions:

1. Brush cabbage with olive oil and grill for 3-4 minutes per side.
2. Shred and toss with onion, carrot, cilantro, lime juice, and salt.

Grilled Pineapple with Tajín

Ingredients:

- 1 pineapple, peeled and sliced into rings
- 1 tablespoon Tajín seasoning
- 1 tablespoon honey (optional)

Instructions:

1. Grill pineapple over medium heat for 2 minutes per side.
2. Sprinkle with Tajín and drizzle with honey if desired.

Barbacoa Tacos with Handmade Tortillas

Ingredients:

For the barbacoa:

- 3 lbs (1.3kg) beef cheek or chuck roast
- 3 dried guajillo chiles, deseeded
- 2 dried ancho chiles, deseeded
- 2 cloves garlic
- 1 teaspoon cumin
- ½ teaspoon oregano
- ½ cup (120ml) vinegar
- 1 teaspoon salt

For the tortillas:

- 2 cups (250g) masa harina
- 1 ¼ cups (300ml) warm water
- ½ teaspoon salt

Instructions:

1. Blend soaked chiles, garlic, cumin, oregano, vinegar, and salt.
2. Coat beef with marinade and smoke at 275°F (135°C) for 5 hours. Shred.
3. Mix masa, water, and salt into a dough. Roll into tortillas and cook on a hot griddle.
4. Fill tortillas with barbacoa and serve.

Quesabirria Tacos (Grilled Birria Tacos with Cheese)

Ingredients:

- 2 lbs (900g) beef chuck
- 3 dried guajillo chiles, deseeded
- 2 dried ancho chiles, deseeded
- 2 cloves garlic
- 1 teaspoon cumin
- ½ teaspoon cinnamon
- ½ teaspoon salt
- 2 cups (480ml) beef broth
- 2 cups (200g) shredded Oaxaca cheese
- 12 corn tortillas

Instructions:

1. Blend soaked chiles, garlic, spices, and broth. Marinate beef overnight.
2. Slow-cook for 4 hours at 275°F (135°C), then shred.
3. Dip tortillas in the birria broth, fill with beef and cheese, and grill until crispy.

Grilled Chicken Wings with Chipotle-Lime Glaze

Ingredients:

- 2 lbs (900g) chicken wings
- 1 teaspoon salt
- ½ teaspoon black pepper

For the glaze:

- 2 chipotle peppers in adobo, minced
- ¼ cup (60ml) lime juice
- 2 tablespoons honey
- 1 teaspoon garlic powder

Instructions:

1. Season wings and grill over medium heat for 20 minutes, flipping occasionally.
2. Mix glaze ingredients and brush onto wings.
3. Grill for 5 more minutes until caramelized.

Mexican BBQ Pork Belly Burnt Ends

Ingredients:

- 3 lbs (1.3kg) pork belly, cubed
- ¼ cup (60ml) honey
- ¼ cup (60ml) chipotle BBQ sauce
- 1 teaspoon smoked paprika
- 1 teaspoon salt

Instructions:

1. Smoke pork belly cubes at 250°F (120°C) for 3 hours.
2. Toss with honey, BBQ sauce, paprika, and salt.
3. Return to smoker for 1 more hour.

Fire-Roasted Chile Relleno

Ingredients:

- 4 poblano peppers
- 1 cup (120g) shredded Oaxaca cheese
- ½ cup (120g) refried black beans (optional)
- 2 eggs, separated
- ½ cup (60g) flour
- Oil for frying

Instructions:

1. Char poblanos on a grill until blackened, then peel.
2. Stuff with cheese and beans, if using.
3. Beat egg whites to stiff peaks, fold in yolks.
4. Coat poblanos in flour, dip in egg batter, and fry until golden.

Smoked Mexican Chorizo Burgers

Ingredients:

- 1 lb (450g) ground beef
- ½ lb (225g) fresh Mexican chorizo, casing removed
- ½ teaspoon salt
- ½ teaspoon black pepper
- 1 teaspoon smoked paprika
- 4 burger buns

For toppings:

- ½ cup (120g) guacamole
- 4 slices pepper jack cheese
- ½ cup (75g) pickled red onions
- ¼ cup (60g) chipotle mayo

Instructions:

1. Preheat smoker to 250°F (120°C).
2. Mix beef, chorizo, salt, black pepper, and smoked paprika. Form into patties.
3. Smoke for 1 hour, then sear on high heat for 2 minutes per side.
4. Serve on buns with guacamole, cheese, pickled onions, and chipotle mayo.

Grilled Sweet Potatoes with Agave Glaze

Ingredients:

- 2 large sweet potatoes, sliced into ½-inch rounds
- 2 tablespoons olive oil
- ¼ cup (60ml) agave syrup
- ½ teaspoon cinnamon
- ½ teaspoon salt

Instructions:

1. Toss sweet potato slices with olive oil and salt.
2. Grill over medium heat for 4-5 minutes per side.
3. Drizzle with agave syrup and sprinkle with cinnamon before serving.

Grilled Watermelon with Chili and Lime

Ingredients:

- 4 large watermelon slices, about 1-inch thick
- 1 tablespoon lime juice
- 1 teaspoon Tajín seasoning
- 1 teaspoon honey (optional)

Instructions:

1. Preheat grill to medium-high heat.
2. Grill watermelon for 1-2 minutes per side until slightly caramelized.
3. Drizzle with lime juice and sprinkle with Tajín.
4. Serve warm with an optional drizzle of honey.

Slow-Smoked Beef Short Ribs with Mexican Spices

Ingredients:

- 3 lbs (1.3kg) beef short ribs
- 2 tablespoons olive oil
- 1 tablespoon salt
- 1 tablespoon black pepper
- 1 teaspoon cumin
- 1 teaspoon smoked paprika
- 1 teaspoon garlic powder
- ½ teaspoon cinnamon

Instructions:

1. Preheat smoker to 250°F (120°C).
2. Rub short ribs with olive oil, then coat with spices.
3. Smoke for 5-6 hours, spritzing with water every hour.
4. Let rest for 15 minutes before serving.

Grilled Mexican Churros

Ingredients:

- 1 cup (240ml) water
- 2 tablespoons butter
- 2 tablespoons sugar
- 1 teaspoon vanilla extract
- 1 cup (125g) all-purpose flour
- 1 teaspoon cinnamon
- 1 egg
- ¼ cup (50g) sugar (for coating)
- Oil for brushing

Instructions:

1. Heat water, butter, and sugar in a pot. Stir in flour and cinnamon until dough forms.
2. Let cool slightly, then mix in egg.
3. Pipe churro shapes onto a greased grill.
4. Grill over medium heat for 2 minutes per side, brushing with oil.
5. Toss in sugar before serving.

Fire-Roasted Plantains with Dulce de Leche

Ingredients:

- 2 ripe plantains, halved lengthwise
- 2 tablespoons butter
- ½ cup (120g) dulce de leche
- ¼ teaspoon cinnamon

Instructions:

1. Brush plantains with butter.
2. Grill over medium heat for 4 minutes per side until caramelized.
3. Drizzle with dulce de leche and sprinkle with cinnamon.

www.ingramcontent.com/pod-product-compliance
Lightning Source LLC
LaVergne TN
LVHW081342060526
838201LV00055B/2796